This Diary Belongs To:

Kelly Dzadu

PRIVATE & CONFIDENTIAL

If found, please return to

ME for REWARD!

ALSO BY

Kelly Dzadu

Me, Myself, & I book 1
Tales from my not so happy
life!!!

Me, Myself, & I book 2
Tales from my new found
popularity!!!

Me, Myself, & I book 2 1/2
All about you!

Me, Myself, & I book 4
Tales from my not so happy
friends deparcure

Kelly Dzadu

Me, Myself, & I

Tales from being a NOT-SO- Glam TV Star

A NOTE TO REMEMBER:

To anyone who has big dreams!

June 20

I'M SO CONFUSED!!!
I can't decide if I need to change my name and
move away, or if I have the BEST little sister in the
world!!
There was this big end-of-school year party in the
park tonight. There were going to be bonfires, a DJ,
and ELIJAH was going to be there. So, of COURSE I
wanted to go. And, of COURSE my parents were all
concerned because it wasn't a school-sponsored
thing and there might not be adults supervising, etc.
The ONLY way they let me go was if they came and
had a picnic with Anastasia on the other side of the
park at the same time.
THE OTHER SIDE OF THE PARK. That was the
bargain. Do you THINK they kept up their end of
it???
It started out okay. My parents dropped me off in the
east parking lot, where I met Justice and Antonise.
They drove around to park in the west parking lot
and I wasn't SUPPOSED to see them again until they
picked me up.
Justice and Antonise had brought chips and soda,
and I had brought marshmallows for roasting, so we
went to drop our food off at the picnic tables first.
Harlisha was there, organizing everything. Some
people were building up the bonfire, and others were
playing with Frisbees and the boy's were playing

football on the lawn. A few kids were at the play area on the equipment. Way on the other side of the play area, I could see my family. Just barely. It was perfect. There were a couple other families over there too, so my parents were not the only ones who'd been all overprotective. (Ugh, PARENTS.)

I was looking around for Elijah when I saw the COMPLETE OPPOSITE of Elijah! Elijah makes my heart happy, gives me butterflies in my stomach, and puts a smile on my face. But INSTEAD, I saw someone who makes my heart sink, gives me slugs in my stomach, and puts a super sour look on my face. That's right...JASMINE!!! Ugh, I mean, it's not like she goes to OHMS any more! But I guess it wasn't a OHMS event. It was just an "end of school year party." So, I guess that includes JASMINE. I was so busy dragging Justice and Antonise away from Jasmine that I guess I didn't notice Anastasia over by the guys with the water balloons. That's right — ANASTASIA! She was totally hanging around a middle school party. I don't know WHAT my parents were thinking!! Supposedly I'm the one they have to worry about, and yet they let their seven-year-old run around and do whatever she wants?!

"What's going on?" Justice asked as I pulled them toward the swings. "Is Elijah over here?"

"No," I said, "but Jasmine's over THERE!"

Right as I said that, Jasmine turned around and looked right at me. She was all the way across the park. There's NO WAY she could have heard me. But she probably has bionic hearing, like some sort of super villain.

And THEN, she started walking toward us. Not walking — STALKING! But she looked kind of goofy because she'd worn high-heeled sandals and they kept sinking into the grass.

"Why is she even coming over here?" Antonise asked. That was exactly what I was thinking!!

It was weird to see Jasmine at a mostly-OHMS party and NOT surrounded by Makayla and her minions. Jasmine walked right up to us and pointed a finger in my face. "You better not have any ideas about coming to Barbizon Hills for Student Exchange Week," she huffed.

LIKE I HAVE ANY CHOICE?!?!

"If you come and open your big mouth about me," she said, "I'll make sure everyone there knows—"

But I don't even know what she was going to threaten me with!! Because right then I heard Anastasia shout, "Kelly, catch!"

We all turned toward her voice just in time to see a water balloon sailing through the air. And then it smacked intoJasmine's HEAD!!!!!!!

I got wet too, but not anywhere nearly as bad as Jasmine. It was kind of brilliant. But the way Jasmine was shrieking, you'd have thought the balloon had been filled with bugs!

I hustled Anastasia back to our parents and we went home soon after that. Elijah wasn't even there, and bringing my family had OBVIOUSLY been a bad idea. It seems like Jasmine is going to try to get even with me!! But at the same time, I'll always have the memory of that water balloon exploding against her perfect hair.

June 21

Last Saturday I went to mentoring and for the day the workshop was about modeling and who knows modeling more than me? I love modeling! I basically live modeling and I would kill t start modeling again! I want to be a model so bad, well sinse my dad introduced me o modeling when I was 7 years old. I have modeled before in not one but 2 PROFFESSIONAL photo shoots! So I kinda have some experience with things like this! And I was so thrilled when Miss. Veronica told me in the morning!

To be continued...

June 22

I just remembered that yesterday was my sister Magdalen's birthday! So, happy birthday to her!

I was too wrapped up in this guess what E! is going to give ME a reality show! I can promise that NO 6'9" athletes will be hurt in the making of MY show!! What will my show be about you ask? And where will the drama come from? Hello! You've been my diary for all this time! You know my life is drama central! Of course I'll have to script it just a little. I'm pretty sure I won't attract millions of viewers with a slow-motion scene of my sisters spilling milk while trying to eat her cereal with their hand friend, Miss Penelope.

And even though the <u>trash-in-the-locker thing</u> was pretty scandalous for my school, I don't think it would bring in the ratings like the hair-pulling brawls you see on those Real Housewives shows. Don't worry...I wouldn't totally sell out or anything! I'd just have to make my life a little more interesting.

So here's what I'm thinking: My sisters will need to have some kind of horrible habit that she's totally in denial about. I think Red Bull would be the best way to go. No, I won't give her actual Red Bull!!

She's already crazy hyper! The last thing she needs is an energy drink!

I'd empty a bunch of cans (because I'm not drinking that stuff either! I read it stunts your growth, and I want to be Tyra's height some day!) Then I'd fill them with apple juice, because it's pretty close to the same color.

BAM: first point of drama for my very own reality show...my impressionable younger sister is throwing her life away on Red Bull!

The next thing a good reality show needs is constant bickering. I actually

like fighting very much. (I'm more the "
We all just get to fighting?!?" type).
So I'm going to ask Justice and Antonise
if they want to pretend they're super
mad at each other when we shoot the
pilot (that means the first ever
episode!)
I'm thinking it can be over some kind of
boy drama. Ooooh! I got it!
Justice can be like, "You've been flirting
with Paul like it's no big deal, and it
makes me sick because he's really your
secret, long-lost brother!"
Everyone likes a secret relative!!
The only other thing I can think of the
top of my head is mom getting pregnant
with sextuplets. But I think that might
take some convincing.
I just want to grab them all by the
shoulders, shake a little sense in them,
and say, "Step away from the
camera!!!"
The competition shows are pretty cool
though. I'm ALL ABOUT Dancing with

the Stars!!
What do you think about reality TV?
Good? Bad? And what shows do you
like?

In the madness of final exams and year-end parties, somehow I forgot!! Every summer my Aunt Christiana takes a road trip with her FIVE KIDS up and down the east coast. They live in Florida, so by the time they get to New York, they have LOST THEIR MINDS.
(If you live in FLORIDA, why would you spend your summer cooped up inside a van? Why wouldn't you just, like, go to the beach?!?!?)
Mom just told us at breakfast that they're coming sometime today. Like... they could be pulling in the driveway right now! Or they might not come until after my sisters are in bed. There's no way to know!! (I mean...you'd THINK they could call us to give us a heads up...but that wouldn't be any fun, WOULD IT??)

THE SUSPENSE IS KILLING ME!!

Visiting cousins might not seem like that big a deal. But let's play a little game. It's called What Did The Dzadu Cousins Do Last Time They Visited???

- Broke every mirror in the house, while playing their game "Mirror Boxing." I AM NOT EVEN KIDDING!!
- Reprogrammed the radio stations in my mom's car so that every single button plays only those soccer comm
- entators screaming "GOOOOOAAALLLLLLLLLLLLLLLLLLLL!!" We haven't listened to anything else in there all year!
- Spilled not one, not two, but ALL FIVE of their Slurpees ON MY BED!! And didn't even tell me! So I went to climb in bed after an exhausting day of t
- heir shenanigans and found a gross, sticky, rainbow swamp where
- my mattress should be!!!
- Explode

-
- ed the giant hippo-shaped beanbag chair in Anastasia's room so that it looked like there'd been a horrible wildlife massacre, an
- d worst of all, those little white foam beads inside went EVERYWHERE! We just stopped digging them out of the carpet last month.

Answer? ALL OF THE ABOVE!!!

After the last visit, Mom suggested we tell them we'd moved. To Alaska. Or Peru. But, Dad said family is family and it could be worse.

How, Dad? HOW??

This is who I'm dealing with:

~~~~12-year-old Sophia — She's younger than me, only she acts like she's about 17 (except when she's punching mirrors and dumping Slurpees in my bed!). She's like a mini-MacKenzie, if MacKenzie were the leader of a biker gang.

~~~~9 year-old Ethan — Ethan is SORT OF okay…when he's sleeping. When he's awake, though, he acts like a puppy who's had a breakfast of chocolate bars, caffeine pills, and soda.

~~~~7-year-old Lucifer — Okay, his name's really Luke. He makes Brianna look like the sweetest, politest, quietest little angel you ever saw. He's the kind of kid who stomps on ants for fun.

~~~~4-year-old twins, Sam and Sam — The twins are seriously named Samuel and Samantha, and they CALL THEM BOTH SAM!!! One of them is ALWAYS screaming and the other one is ALWAYS crying. But they mix it up, just to keep you guessing.

And then there's Aunt Christiana. She floats through the house, oblivious to the crazy, and once I heard her ask my mom if she's at all concerned about MY social development. I had just run through the room carrying all the underwear I own, but I HAD MY REASONS!

So, now I'm brainstorming everything I can do to protect my stuff/my house/my family before they get here. Mom says I'm not allowed to run away and hide at Chloe's or Zoey's, AND I'm not allowed to barricade my door shut. But she didn't say anything about my sisters doors, so right now my plan is to stuff all my valuables under my sister's bed and make she's not in the room when I barricade her door!

June 25

I was TOTALLY prepared for the arrival
of my crazy Dzadu cousins. I'd hidden
my valuables. Justice and I were on
standby to brainstorm escape routes via
text. Elijah even said I could come
volunteer at Fuzzy Friends if things got
too crazy around here!
When their van pulled up, I got super
sweaty. Was I REALLY ready? Could I
handle another WEEK of Dzadu cousin
madness??? What would they
destroy?? Would the house still be
standing when they left?
MOST horrifying thought: Would my
sisters learn NEW ways to make my life
miserable????
Aunt Christiana got out of the van. She
stretched, came up the walk, and
hugged my dad. But, my cousins stayed
in the car.

Then, my dad asked about the kids and Aunt Christiana waved her hand like she barely remembered she had kids. "Oh...they're still in the car."

They eventually came into the house, but it was the WEIRDEST THING. It was like the Dzadu cousins had been body snatched!! Like alien pod people had come down in the night and beamed them up to their planet (good luck, alien planet!!!) and then aliens had taken over the Dzadu cousin bodies!

And those aliens didn't seem to be able to do anything except stare at screens!!!

One by one, they shuffled out of the car and into the house, eyes glued to screens. Inside, they each found a corner and sat. QUIETLY!!!!

I did not know WHAT was going on!!

Sophia, who's 12, was listening to music while doing stuff on her phone. When I tried to say hi, she acted like she didn't hear me!! Which...she probably didn't!

Ethan and Luke, 9 and 7, were both

playing games on tablets. But not, like, against each other. Each in their own world. QUIET!!! I really can't explain how quiet they all were!!! It was FREAKING ME OUT!!!

Finally, Sam and Sam, the four-year-old twins, were sharing a tablet and watching some cartoon. When Magdalen asked if she could watch, they took the headphones out and let her. But she got bored of hunching over a little screen after a while.

"What's wrong with them, Kelly?" she asked me.

"I don't know." At first, it was freaky, sure. But I wasn't complaining. Maybe I could act like they weren't here at all! But after a couple days I could see that was NOT going to work. Because they WERE here. They were EVERYWHERE I wanted to sit. There was NO hot water. And, my favorite cereal was always gone by the time I got up.

WORST of all, my sisters had gotten

used to hunching over the little screen
with Sam and Sam, so THEY had turned
into screen aliens too!! It wasn't that I
WANTED them to bug me. But they was
FREAKING me out!!!
So I took DRASTIC ACTION.
While they were all screen-staring, I
crept around and dug through their
backpacks and suitcases. I'm not exactly
PROUD of this, but I did feel kind of
like a secret agent. I found each of their
charger cords, put them all in a bag, and
put the bag in the glove compartment
of their van.
Then I waited.
The twins were the first to lose power.
When their mom couldn't find the cord
for them, the screaming began. I
considered being the hero who
discovered all the cords. Together. In
the van. It would have been pretty hard
to explain.
When Ethan couldn't find his charger,
he decided he was going to invent his

own, using whatever he could find. This included pipe cleaners, aluminum foil, candy bar wrappers, and string. This was entertaining, until I realized he was planning to stick the pipe cleaners into the electric socket. I convinced him to make it a solar-powered charger, so he took that project outside.

PHEW!

Luke's response to losing power AND his charger was to go full King Kong all over the living room, knocking pillows to the ground, tipping over the coffee table, kicking the couch, etc. The upside of this was that Sam & Sam stopped screaming and joined in the destruction. My mom and I ran around making sure breakable things didn't get knocked off of shelves. It was stressful, but hey! At least something was HAPPENING.

Sophia was the last to run out of power. She narrowed her heavily lined eyes at me. "It's kind of suspicious that NONE

of us can find our chargers," she said.
I grinned. "Weird, right?"
And then I threw a pillow at her head.
Yes, I feel a little guilty about what I did.
But, I like my loud and crazy cousins
better than my quiet zombie cousins!

June 27

Don't mind me, just hiding from a pack of six-year-olds.

Hiding isn't the right word.

Cowering? Figuring out how I might disguise myself and escape this house? It all started when Anastasia watched the old animated Disney version of Alice in Wonderland. I tried to warn her not to. That creepy cat gave me nightmares for years. But Anastasia didn't care about the cat. NOPE, she's fixated on the Unbirthday Song. She played it over and over. Sung it at the dinner table. On the toilet. In her sleep. "A VERY MERRY UNBIRTHDAY TO YOU! TO ME? TO YOU!" I seriously considered lugging the TV up to the roof and dropping it off. My mom apparently felt the same way, because she made a deal with Anastasia: if she would STOP SINGING THAT SONG, Mom would throw her an unbirthday party of her very own!! SO UNFAIR, right?? Anastasia annoys her way into a PARTY????

My mom tried to tell me it wasn't really a party. There wouldn't be a cake or presents. It would really just be a playdate with a bunch of kids.

But there are balloons and streamers and cupcakes (which are TINY CAKES, MOM!!!!). Mom tried to bribe me into helping with the party (which wasn't a party...except it totally was). And okay...it worked. She offered to let me go to this big hip hop music festival that Harlisha's dad has backstage passes to,

but my mom had said no way, I was too young. So I hung in there as long as I could. I filled up water guns, I poured punch, I cleaned up spilled punch, I showed kids to the bathroom, I ran the music. I was EARNING that music festival. But then Anastasia wanted me to play The Unbirthday Song. But the WHOLE POINT of the party was that I would never have to hear that song again! "But it's my unbirthday party!!" she wailed. "We HAVE to play the song!!!" I mean, I got it. On principle. But also? The whole party was because she'd agreed NOT to sing the song anymore!! So I refused. It was maybe not the wisest choice I could have made. Anastasia might look all sweet and innocent to outsiders, but she's kind of an evil genius. She told all her little friends that I was hiding a HUGE stash of candy somewhere in the house, and if they followed me everywhere I went and asked for clues, I would lead them to it. I didn't know WHAT she'd said. I just knew that suddenly they were all following me around and saying things like, "Where's the candy?" "Hot or cold?" "Upstairs or downtairs?" "If you tell me, I'll be your best friend!" Excuse me, but I already HAVE two BFFs and they do NOT bug me for candy all day!!!
When I FINALLY figured out what was happening, I told everyone we were going out in the backyard to play tag. I thought this would distract them! They would have to run away from whoever was it! They would forget about ME! But remember how I said Anastasia is an evil genius? She started handing out the water guns and telling everyone that whoever

hit me the MOST times would get the candy! It made ZERO sense! If I was the keeper of the candy, why would I give it to people spraying me?!

But newsflash: six-year-olds don't care a whole lot about what makes sense! If someone gives them a water gun and says, "GET HER!" they just start shooting!

I finally made it inside, where my mom started yelling at me about running through the house dripping wet, but then she got distracted by all the kids trying to follow me inside with water guns. That gave me enough time to lock myself in my room. So here I am and here I'll stay until every single maniac six-year-old has left this house! Except Anastasia. I guess I'm stuck with her. And if my mom tries to say I can't go the music festival because I didn't help for the whole party, you know what I'm going to do?

Start. Singing.

June 28

OMG!! Today I had the biggest fashion dilemma
EVER in the history of the WORLD!!!
The week had been unbelievably HOT and our A/C
broke. Mom and Dad said it wasn't "ecologically
responsible" to drive around and around in the car
with the A/C on. I was SO HOT I would have even
been okay driving in Dad's roach-mobile!!
But noooo, suddenly my parents were
environmentalists or something!
So when my mom suggested we go to the community
pool, I ignored the reasons I usually say no.
(Overcrowded, screaming toddlers and pee in the
pool, to start.) I said fine and my sisters danced
around so much I got hotter just watching them.
But when I went to grab my new swimsuit, I couldn't
find it!! I searched EVERYWHERE!!
It wasn't in my drawers or my closet. It wasn't under
my bed. It wasn't in the laundry room.
"Tick tock, Kelly," my mom said, when I asked her if
she'd seen it. "If we don't get there early, we won't
get in."
I tried to remember the last time I'd seen my bathing
suit, but I couldn't!
"You can wear one of mine," my mom said.
I almost DIED. First of all, one of my mom's suits
would NOT fit me. And even if they would, they'd be
way too old lady! (No offense to my mom. But she's
not exactly a fashion icon.)

I was searching through the very back of my closet when my mom appeared in my doorway. "I've had this since before I had kids," she said, with a sort of faraway look in her eyes. "I always hoped it would fit me again, but somehow I don't think so."

She tossed it on my bed and snapped, "Now, hurry up and let's go." I was almost afraid to look. But I was also sweating through my shorts and tank top. A swimming pool sounded like heaven right about then...

I looked.

OMG. My mom's suit was leopard print...but not regular, like black and tan, leopard. It was NEON purple and NEON orange leopard print!

Things only got more confusing from there. I couldn't figure out whether it was a one-piece or a two-piece. It all held together in one piece when I picked it up, but there were way more holes than I knew what to do with.

When I finally got it on, I stared in horror at the mirror. It fit...I guess? But it was like the bathing suit couldn't decide whether it wanted to be a one-piece or a two-piece. It was all connected like a one piece, but it had this giant cutout in the stomach and the middle of the back. The 1980's had come to haunt me and I would be forever scarred.

"Yikes," Magdalen said from the doorway.

I almost went over and slammed the door in her face, but she was holding out a suit, too. For a second I thought maybe she'd found mine.

"You can wear this one," she said. "I stretched it out too much playing tug of war with Daisy."

I sighed. It couldn't be worse than Mom's Technicolor leopard monstrosity. Could it?

I put it on and...it depends how you define worse. It was a little tight. And faded. And linty. And it had My Little Ponies all over it. Plus a ruffle on the butt. I only had a minute to decide, because by this time, Mom was honking from the driveway.

I grabbed my towel and headed for the door. I figured it was sort of...retro? In a better way than Mom's suit, which was ACTUALLY retro.

So, now we're in the car on the way to the pool and I'm just keeping my fingers crossed I don't see ANYONE I know!!! Otherwise, I'm going to be known as Pony Ruffle Butt forever!!

June 30

Sometimes I wonder if my mom sleeps
with her eyes open when I talk because
it's like she doesn't know me AT ALL!!
The other day she was all like, "I'm so
proud of you for doing well on your
Math test!" And that's kind of random
since I actually got a 35 because I was
super tired that day!! Maybe she just
assumed I did well because she wanted
me to?
Anywho, she was like, "Since you did SO
well I think we should go to Target and
buy you some new pajamas!"
Um, really? THAT'S my reward for doing
well?? I know, I didn't actually deserve
a reward at all...but if I did, I definitely
wouldn't want Target flannels as a
reward!
Then later that night, she was like, "How
would you feel about having professional

pictures taken, just the two of us?"
I guess there's some online group where mothers post pictures of themselves with their daughters. I mean, it's sweet that she wants to be close with me and all. And I love her and everything, I really do.
But there's NO WAY I would want pictures of the two of us posted all over the web!
I mean I can just see it now: The two of us in matching sweater vests, doing cheesy pose with our chins on our fists. I might as well just email everyone in my school and say "Please, cyber bully me now!"
Then my mom was like, "Do you think I should make a profile on the Instagram? We could be friends!" (I don't have a personal page, but I have one for my books...in case you haven't seen it, it's here!)
But really...Instagram?? We should NOT be friends on Instagram!

Then the other day, she came to school to pick me up and asked if we should give my friend Jessica a ride.

Jessica is SO not my friend!! If we gave her a ride, she'd probably plant some type of bugging device in the car so she could spy on us and collect dirt for Jasmine.

OK so I guess I could tell my mom a little more about my life and stuff. Then maybe she wouldn't seem so clueless. But sometimes it feels like she's from a different planet or something.

I think she kind of feels bad because my sisters take a ton of her time. Those girls needs attention 24/7!!

And if my mom's trying to talk with me about anything, one of them does something totally crazy or bratty to pull her away.

Like the other day, my mom was asking me what I was going to cook for dinner. (Because Monday's my night to cook now.)

She told me she wanted to show me how to make her special lasagna, but then Anastasia started going, "Mooom! Moooom! Mooooooooom!"
Like just saying it over and over again. SO annoying!
Mom was like, "Just a minute hun. I'm helping Kelly!"
Then the next thing you know, Anastasia's crying because she was dancing around in the living room and she knocked this vase over and broke it. So of course my mom had to run over to make her feel better. That was SO not an accident!!!
So my Mom was like, "Kelly could you use these pieces for some kind of art project?" Okay, I admit that was a kind of cool idea.
Maybe she knows me a little after all. But I'm SO not doing LAME mother-daughter photos!!!

July 10

Omg, something horrible in the history of life has happened to me. I lost my black pen! This is not just any pen its my pen that I borrowed from Elijah. Anyway while I am going to find it later there is something so important to talk about. As you know school is back in session on Aug 23 and that means all the drama with these dumb girls are going to start againg and I'm not sure if this year I will be as tough as I was last school year. I mean me and Jasmine got into a fist fish and I don't think that this year fighting is going to help me I might get a tooth knocked out. I just have to only use my fist when I need them this school year. I have to make a promise to myself. I KELLY DIAMOND DECLAIR ON THIS DAY NOT TO USE MY FIST TO DO ANYTHING THIS YEAR UNLESS

I OR MY FAMILY MEMBER OR MY FRIENDS ARE IN DANGER, I PROMISE!!!

July 11

I've written a ton recently about how much I LOVE the summer, but there's one thing that's SO not cool...I don't get to see Elijah every day!

I mean I suppose I COULD see him every day, but I think his family would get pretty concerned if I walked around their front door several times each afternoon, like I walk by his locker in school!

(OK, I don't walk by his locker a few times EVERY day...I'm not a stalker or anything!)

We haven't really talked on the phone a ton (and come to think of it...whenever he's called me, I've been in the bathroom and Anastasia's humiliated me!)

It's not like we're a couple or anything. But I definitely want to keep in touch over the summer, and maybe even hang out and stuff.

I just don't know how to do it!

Maybe I could find out his Skype name so I can be all casual online some day, like, "Hey stranger...how's your summer going?!?"

Except with less punctuation. I don't want to look like I'm crazy overexcited to talk to him!

But if I just see him online and we start casually chatting, we could chat kind of regularly. We could be Skype buddies! Then one day I could be like, "OMG I'm SO bored today! I wanted to go ride my bike with Justice and Harlisha, but they're sick."

Then he'd be like, "BOTH of them?"

And I'd realize I'm not a good liar. LOL! But then he'd ask, "Want to go ride bikes with me?"

And then we could hang out all afternoon! We could get pizza for lunch and maybe even go see a movie too.

Wow, that would be like a real date!
I don't think we're really THERE yet, but
I definitely feel a lot closer to him after
everything that happened with the
animal shelter and the ice skating
competition!
OMG I just had a GREAT idea! So
remember I had that garage sale a
while back and made a TON of cash?
(No? OK) I was thinking that maybe I'd
go through some of my stuff and sell
more of it. Last time I found all these
lame reasons to keep things I never use.
(Like, I can't sell these old pink bunny
slippers. So what if I never wear them?
Maybe someday I'll want to make a
bunny costume for a doll, and these will
come in handy!)
Anyways, I was thinking that maybe I'd
sell my stuff on Amazon instead of
doing a garage sale, with my Mom's
help...and I'll need really good pictures
of all my stuff.
I could totally ask Elijah to help with

that! He's SUCH an awesome photographer, and I know he loves helping people out. (He's SO sweet!!!) So now it's just a matter of WHEN I'll do this. I'll want him to come over when my sisters aren't here. If they are home, I just KNOW they will talk his ear off...! Maybe I can get Mom to stay outside in the kiddie pool with them. So I should probably do it on a super hot day when I know they will want to swim. (And by swim, I mean sit in a foot of water... that pool is SO tiny!!)

BRB...phone!

Back! So that was harlisha, and she thinks I have an AWESOME idea. Squeeeeee!! I can't wait to see Elijah again. School just ended recently and it already feels like way too long.

JULY 12

Squeeeeee!!!! That's my being totally psyched because Elijah came over my house this weekend!

I asked my big sister to hang with my sisters outside so they wouldn't drive us bonkers. I had this horrible dream on Friday that they totally RUINED Elijah's visit. In my dream, he knocked on the door, and then Anastasia answered it and dragged him up to her room.

Since I didn't hear him knocking, I kept acting like he wasn't there yet.

I didn't have any clean underwear, so I ran to the laundry room to see if maybe my mom washed some, but she didn't. So I started screaming, "Mom!!!! I don't have any clean underwear!!"

Then Anastasia skipped in holding hands with Elijah, and said, "Kelly, Elijah's here! He's SO nice! He doesn't care if you're wearing dirty underwear!!"

I woke up covered in sweat. Thank GOD that was just a dream!! I'd be SO embarrassed if that happened in real life!

Unlike in my dream, Elijah rang the doorbell when he got there, and my little sisters were outside in the kiddie pool.

My dad got to the door first and had a "Man to Boy talk" Before I went downstairs, I sprayed myself with my mom's perfume. But I accidentally put WAY too much on.

I don't usually wear perfume, so I thought it was like hairspray...and sometimes I need A LOT of hairspray! When I When I went down stairs and met Elijah , he started to cough a little. Then he said, "Did you just get some flowers?" I didn't want him to know I practically took a shower in my mom's floral-scented perfume because I wanted to impress him, so I said, "Um, yeah. And I tripped and fell on them. I'm

such a klutz!" That was kind of awkward! Before he came, I brought all the stuff I want him to photograph down into the living room because my mom had said, "Keep Elijah downstairs. It's a MESS upstairs. It looks like a TORNADO went through it!"
But he was like, "Want to give me a tour?"
It's pretty hard to give someone a tour when you can't show them half of your house, but I did my best!
First I brought him into the kitchen, and said, "So this is our kitchen."
Then he said, "I figured. The oven and fridge gave it away!"
He's so funny!
After that I brought him back to the living room and said, "The upstairs is pretty much like this, but higher up, without the appliances. Want to get started?"
I thought that was a pretty good cover!
He started taking pictures of my stuff

while I pretty much just stood there and tried to make small talk.

About 10 minutes in I had to go to the bathroom. I was only in there for like a minute, but that minute was WAY too long! When I came back out, I saw Anastasia dripping wet, drawing on Elijah's hand!

I asked her in a SUPER nice way to stay outside, but I should have known she couldn't resist!

I was like, "Hey there sis...what are you doing?" I sounded pretty calm, but I was FUMING inside!

Then she went, "I'm drawing on Elijah duh are you bling or something?."

And then Elijah said, "She's funny." Aww me and Elijah are bonding! It sounded so cute when ELijah said "She's funny!

After that Anastasia kind of surprised me. She said, "I'll leave you two alone!" Then she giggled and ran back outside. I was actually kind of glad she came in for a bit. She may be kind of nutty sometimes, but I love that little nut ball, and it's kind of nice to see Elijah being so sweet to her.

After that, Elijah finished taking the pictures, and then said he had to go to the animal shelter.

And get this...he asked me if I wanted to come! I already had plans with Harlisha and Justice so I had to say no. (I'd never ditch them to hang out with a boy...even if it's an awesome boy like Elijah!) He said, "Maybe next weekend then." He SO wants to see me a lot over the summer! Looks like I was worried for nothing.

July 16

The beach is SUPER FUN when it's really warm out, but it SO wasn't yesterday!!
I was Facetiming with Harlisha in the morning and I was like,
"Squeeeeeeeee!!!! It's the summer. Let's go to the beach!!!"
Harlisha wanted to just chill and watch movies instead, because she was not sure if the weather was going to be nice enough for the beach.
But I REALLY, REALLY, REALLY, REALLY wanted to go!
I mean, I DREAM about the beach all through the school year! Seriously, I draw little sketches of me eating ice cream while sitting on a stone wall, playing volleyball with a bunch of super cute boys, and riding my bike in a totally cute bathing suit and jean shorts.
That's what summer's all about...not sitting around watching movies!!

OK, so to be fair, watching movies is also a pretty cool summer activity. Any time you're not in school AND with your friends, it's a pretty awesome day!
But you can't get a suntan when you're laying on your couch in your living room, and you DEFINITELY can't swim.
So I talked them into going. I was like, "I PROMISE you'll have a great time!"
I spent like FOREVER picking out the bathing suit I was going to wear, which is even sadder since I only own three of them (I DEFINITELY need to get that cute yellow one I want ASAP!)
Then I filled this super huge beach bag with all my beach essentials:
- Sunscreen (Yeah, I know I said I like get
- ting tanned...but I also like NOT getting sun blisters!)
- A HUGE towel
- 2 magazines (One for each of us!)
- 2 Snapples (One for each o
- f us

-
- s!)
- 2 ham-and-cheese (One for each of us!)
- 2 Hershey bars (You get the point!)

It's super important that you NEVER bring tuna sandwiches to the beach, because they end up smelling NASTY like a fish sticks dipped in sewage.

I know you might be thinking the chocolate bar thing isn't too smart since it will most likely melt. Au contraire! (That's how the French say "Nu uh.")

A melted candy bar comes in super handy if you want to buy the cheapest ice cream at the store and then squeeze it on top for a Sundae!

Anyway, I was ALL ready for the beach! I heard Harlisha's aunt beeping her horn outside. Then I looked out my window and saw Harlisha in the car.

I was SO psyched they were going to pick me up, so we could go RIGHT to the beach from my house! I practically skipped to the car...that's how excited I was!

But right when my hand touched the handle, guess what happened?

It started POURING rain! It was like a torrential downpour, just out of nowhere. No warning drops or anything!

I opened the door and jumped inside anyway...it was a lot closer than running back to my house!

Then Harlisha looked at me and said, "Movies?"

I had a feeling it was going to rain at some point (not because I'm psychic....because the weather man said there was a chance!) But I guess I didn't want to believe it.

We ended up chilling at my house, watching movies, and looking at cute bathing suits online, all while I plotted ways to get my mom to buy me a new one in my head.

We didn't get to splash around in the

water or lay on the sand, but we had fun anyway, and hey, there was another silver lining...
Our candy didn't melt!

July 18

This past weekend was CRAZY!! I babysit my sisters on Saturday night, and they totally drove me NUTS!

Before Mom and Dad left, they were like, "Be good to your sisters! Don't just lock them in their room with a movie on so you can Facetime with Harlisha!"

I was all like, "I'd NEVER do that!! What kind of a heartless big sister do they think I am??"

I put the movie on in the LIVING ROOM and I Facetimed chatted with ROYRIE instead!

I got *Tangled* from Netflix. I thought they would be psyched! I just wanted a few minutes to myself, and then I had some cool arts and crafts stuff planned for us.

I was chatting with Royrie in my room for all of FIVE minutes when Anastasia screamed my name.

She was like, "Kelllllly! Kelllllllyyyyy! Kelllllllllyyyyy!" Why do kids always drag out the first syllable of your name? And why on earth do they yell it like 50 million times in a row instead of giving you a chance to respond??

I knew she probably wanted me to hang out with them, so I told Royrie I was going to chill with them for a bit and then I'd talk to her later.

When I walked into the living room, I saw that Anastasia was trying to glue a bunch of yarn to her hair so she could look like Rapunzel.

She must have heard me talking about glue-in hair extensions the other day and thought it would be a good idea. It SO wasn't!!

Her head was like a HUGE rat's nest! I had no idea what to do to get it out! I tried to comb through it with some leave-in detangler but she kept screaming, "Stop it!! You're hurting me!" And, "I'm missing the movie!!"

So I was like, "FINE! But when the movie's over, you have to sit still so I can fix your hair!"

I was so mad at myself for being in the other room. Sometimes I forget you have to keep your eye on Anastasia literally ALL the time or she'll get into major trouble!

We started to watch the movie for a bit. I was on the floor lying on my stomach with a pillow, and she was on the couch behind me. I turned around at one point because she was kind of quiet, and I saw she was trying to climb up the bookcase next to the couch.

So of course I flipped out! And she was like, "I'm RAPUNZEL! I need a TOWER! Duh!"

Luckily I got her down without the whole thing toppling all over. She's SO lucky I was there to save her from death by bookcase!

After the movie, I went online to figure out how I could fix her hair.

Some people suggested using nail polish remover, some said peanut butter, some people said olive oil, and other people said a TON of hair conditioner.

So I tried all of it! I had her head in the kitchen sink, and she kept flailing around, which made a TOTAL mess of the kitchen!

I couldn't get it out, so eventually I had to call my Mom and Dad. They were SUPER annoyed that I let this happen!

They had to come home early, and my dad even said, "I'm disappointed in you Kelly."

That made me feel horrible. I HATE when parents say they're disappointed in you!

Next time I'm not taking my eyes off those girls for even a second. In fact, I might even get one of those backpacks with a leash on it, so I can make sure they NEVER leave my sight!

August 25

OMG!! I had the most amaaaaaaazing day ever!!!!!!

Okay, so Makayla's dad is a record executive (records are how music used to be played, before the world got CIVILIZED—basically, he works in the music industry). And it took some arm-twisting, but I got my parents to say YES when Makayla invited me to this super amazing music festival that's been sold out for MONTHS.

When we got the festival, Makayla's dad handed us each these passes on necklaces that said ALL ACCESS.

"These mean you can go anywhere here at the festival?" he said. "There are four different stages, and you can get into general seating for all of them."

"Can we go backstage, Daddy?"

Makayla asked.

I hadn't even THOUGHT of that!! I might get to meet Fetty Wap, DJ Khaled, and Kelly Rowland! And the biggest headliner of the festival!! OMG!!

But he shook his head. "Sorry, sweetheart. The bands control backstage access. Have fun. Keep your phones on. Answer my texts when I check in. Got it?"

Then he hurried off to do whatever record executives do at a music festival. Royrie, Makyla, and I looked at each other, and then all around us. Then, all together we screamed, "OMG!!!!!"

We huddled around Makayla's phone to look at the schedule and decided to head to the main stage to stake out good seats for Fetty Wap show starting in half an hour.

They were AMAZING. So were the Fetty Wap and DJ Khaled!!

By the time it started to get dark, we'd already had more fun than I thought I

could have ALL SUMMER. We sent
selfies to our friends, ate TONS of junk
food, and danced so hard my feet were
about to fall off. And Kelly Rowland
hadn't performed yet!!!!

We got to his show WAY early and
collapsed on the grass. I didn't think
anything could ruin that moment. But
then something did. Or SOMEONE.

"OMG, are you KIDDING me?" said the
most annoying voice in the world.
(No, NOT my sisters pretending to be
Princess Sugar Plum. Even WORSE!!!)

JASMINE was standing there, hands on
hips, sneering at us in our matching t-
shirts. "What are YOU losers doing
here?? I thought this festival was
supposed to be exclusive."

Royrie recovered from her shock first.
Then, she replied, "I'll have you know,
THIS LOSER"—she pointed at Makayla
—"has a father in the music business!"

MacKenzie snorted while Royrie told
Makayla she didn't mean that like it

sounded.

"Whatever." Jasmine huffed. "Are THOSE your seats?"

OBVIOUSLY, they were our seats. Our stuff was all spread out.

I rolled my eyes. "Where are you sitting, Jasmine? On the stage??"

She sniffed. "That wouldn't be the best view. No, I'm in the VIP seats. IN THE FRONT ROW. Have fun, LOSERS. If you can't see Kelly from here, maybe I'll post some videos on my YouTube channel later."

We tried not to let Jasmine put a damper on our fun. But, it was SUCH a bummer knowing she was there, and in the FRONT ROW!!!

Just a couple minutes before the show started, Makayla got a text from her dad.

"Daddy says we need to meet him down by the exit at the side of the stage," she said.

Royrie frowned. "It's filling up. If we

leave our seats now, we'll lose them!"

"Yeah," Makayla said, "but if we don't do what he says, he won't get us in the next time he's got tickets to something like this."

So, we packed up our stuff and trudged down by the stage. It was a let down, since Kelly was the singer we were MOST excited about seeing.

When we got down there, Mr. Franklin stepped out of a little door we hadn't even noticed, which looked like it led backstage.

"Hi Daddy," Makayla said. "Do we have to leave now?"

And THEN, from behind Mr. Franklin, came another voice.

"Leave? But my show hasn't even started yet!"

And THEN Kelly Rowland stepped out!!!!

SQUEEEEE!!!!!

"Are you Makayla?" she said. "And Makayla's friends? Kelly and Royrie,

right?"
OMG OMG OMG OMG OMG OMG
OMG!!!!
"Kelly has just signed with my label," Mr. Franklin said. "And she thought you guys might like to come hang out in her dressing room during her opening act!" Just as people behind us started to notice Kelly standing in plain sight, Mr. Franklin motioned us into the little hallway. I turned around to see Jasmine gaping at us and gave her a little wave. "Maybe I'll post a video later." I shouted to Jasmine. "But probably not!"

September 28

So, today I started going out with this boy named Kayden this cute ass boy that I think loves me and I don't know if people are going to be so happy about me and him being together. Amariee made me scared by saying that Micheal was going to fight Kayden and Kayden is kinda buff (really strong)and I'm sorry but Micheal just might get his ass WHOPPED. He's just omg so cute. (Kayden I mean) I don't know why I waited to ask him out. Actually I know just why I waited Ma'Kaiya said that he had a girlfriend and I belived the little bitch. Ugh she is so annoying god dang. Why would she lie? unless...... she auctually liked him I mean think about it . What is the reason why you would tell your freind that the boy she likes is taken by a different boy. I mean thats rediculause. I'm so mad towards her. She hasn't been in school the whole week and when she comes back I will so give her a peice of my mind but first I have to fix what is or may happen with Micheal and my new boyfriend Kayden (man I love saying the word boyfriend) I love him though. I would so kiss him but I don't know if he is that kind of boy. Anyway to stay on topic I don't want for Kayden to get suspended, same goes for Micheal I care about both of them so much it just so happens that I go out with Kayden. Then theres this problem with Makayla that she said I like her boyfriend Fernando (changed his name) and I don't I mean why would I when I like and devote myself to someone (Kayden) and I love him. Anyway on the other hand William and Brendi started going out today isn't that so sweet? I know it is. I'm still mad at Ma'Kaiya

September 29

Omg tommorow we have no school. But guess who didn't want to come to school? You guessed it Kayden. I was so sad the whole day because when you have a boyfriend to go to school to you just want to go everyday and just be there with them so bad. But he didn't come to school and I went to school looking all good. Man I was so mad. But you know where Kayden isn't Micheal is. He likes me so much but I don't even like him in that way. I just wanna be friends with him. I do really want I and Kayden to work out. Makayla is still not talking to me I REALLY DON'T CARE but as far as she knows I do and that drives her so crazy and omg that is so funny. So I'm still going to not comfront her. Or Allazia. But that's another story that I will get into now. Allazia is mad at me because supposedly I looked at her some type of way. And I don't even remember doing that. Tommorow I have to wake up I have to go to the dentist.

Use the next pages to write your own adventures.

My name is Kelly Dzadu. I am 13 years old. I go to Oxon Hill Middle school. I love to play and be goofy. When I am at home

and I'm not writing a
book or something I
just like to be a normal
13 year old girl!

Pretty
NO PR

CHECK OUT M

we

@WWW.kDmemyseLf

MYSELF, & I'S

ITE

DIBOOKS.WEEBLY.COM

Lightning Source UK Ltd.
Milton Keynes UK
UKHW020650110619
344160UK00009B/135/P

9 781366 548979